To My Wonderful Aunt, I Want to Hear Your Story

An Aunt's
Guided Journal
To Share Her Life &
Her Love

Jeffrey Mason

Hear Your Story Books

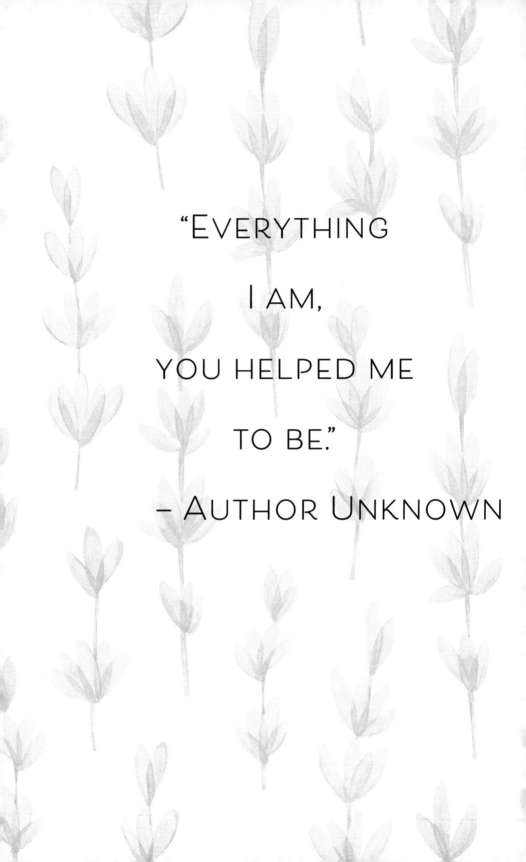

"Everything

I am,

you helped me

to be."

– Author Unknown

This Book

Holds & Shares

The Life Stories of:

_____

_____

"ONLY AN AUNT
CAN GIVE HUGS
LIKE A MOTHER,
KEEP SECRETS
LIKE A SISTER AND
SHARE LOVE
LIKE A FRIEND."
- AUTHOR UNKNOWN

About This Book

"The thing that interests me most about family history
is the gap between the things we think we know
about our families and the realities." – Jeremy Hardy

Our families are our connections to what came before
and what comes after. They show us the magnificence of
what can happen when we set aside our own needs, ignore
our differences, and allow ourselves to join with others.

Our connections with each other are strengthened when
we hear and understand each other's life stories, and
"To My Wonderful Aunt, I Want to Hear Your Story"
provides a place for some of the best storytellers of all
to share their lives and their experiences.

Hearing who they are and where they have been allows
us to see them in new ways.

We see them as girls growing into young women and as
women holding on to some of who they were as little
girls. We see their stumbles and their triumphs, and we
learn from their challenges and their chosen paths.

We see how alike we are, we better understand and
empathize, and we develop new perspectives on our
differences, beliefs, and judgments.

To My Wonderful Aunt, I Want to Hear Your Story is a
book dedicated to the timeless and sacred art of passing
on, sharing, and learning from the collective stories of
our families.

IT'S YOUR BIRTHDAY!
"Great sisters get promoted to aunt."
— Author Unknown

What is your birthdate?

_____

What was your full name at birth?

_____

Were you named after a relative or someone else of significance?

_____

_____

_____

In what city were you born?

_____

What was your length and weight at birth?

_____

Were you born in a hospital? If not, where?

_____

_____

What were your first words?

_____

_____

IT'S YOUR BIRTHDAY!

"Each of us is tomorrow's ancestors."
— Author Unknown

How old were you when you started to walk?

_____

How old were your parents when you were born?

_____

_____

How did your parents describe you as a baby?

_____

_____

_____

_____

_____

_____

_____

_____

_____

_____

IT'S YOUR BIRTHDAY!

"The great use of life is to spend it for
something that will outlast it." — William James

What stories have you been told about the day you were
born?

_____

_____

_____

_____

_____

_____

_____

_____

_____

_____

_____

_____

_____

IT'S YOUR BIRTHDAY!
"To forget one's ancestors is to be a brook without
a source, a tree without a root." — Chinese Proverb

What is a favorite childhood memory?

_____

_____

_____

_____

_____

_____

_____

_____

_____

_____

_____

_____

_____

WHAT HAPPENED
THE YEAR YOU WERE BORN?

"An aunt is someone special to remember with warmth,
think of with pride and cherish with love." — Author Unknown

Google the following for the year you were born:
What are some notable events that occurred?

_____

_____

_____

_____

_____

What movie won the Academy Award for Best Picture? Who
won for Best Actor and Best Actress?

_____

_____

_____

What were a few popular movies that came out that year?

_____

_____

_____

_____

_____

WHAT HAPPENED
THE YEAR YOU WERE BORN?

"The most important thing in the
world is family and love." — John Wooden

What song was on the top of the Billboard charts?

_____

Who was the leader of the country (President, Prime
Minister, etc.)?

_____

What were a few popular television shows?

_____

_____

_____

_____

_____

What were the prices for the following items?
- A loaf of bread:
- A gallon of milk:
- A cup of coffee:
- A dozen eggs:
- The average cost of a new home:
- A first-class stamp:
- A new car:
- A gallon of gas:
- A movie ticket:

7

GROWING UP

"A family doesn't have to be perfect; it just needs to be united."
— Author Unknown

How would you describe yourself when you were a kid?

_____

_____

_____

_____

Did you have a nickname when you were growing up? If yes, how did you get it?

_____

Who were your best friends in your elementary school days? Are you still in contact with them?

_____

_____

_____

_____

What were your regular chores? Did you get an allowance? How much was it and what did you spend it on?

_____

_____

_____

GROWING UP
"Life is really simple, but we insist on making it complicated."
— Confucius

Describe what your room looked like when you were growing up. Was it messy or clean? Did you have paintings or posters on the walls? What were the main colors?

_____

_____

_____

_____

_____

_____

_____

_____

What is one thing you miss about being a kid?

_____

_____

_____

_____

TRIVIA
"Of all the things my hands have held, the best, by far, is you."
— Author Unknown

What is your favorite flavor of ice cream?

_____

How do you like your coffee?

_____

_____

If you could live anywhere in the world for a year with all expenses paid, where would you choose?

_____

_____

_____

How do you like your eggs cooked?

_____

Preference: cook or clean?

_____

What is your shoe size?

_____

What superpower would you choose for yourself?

_____

_____

TRIVIA

"Aunts make life a little sweeter."
— Author Unknown

Do you have any allergies?

_____

_____

_____

What is your biggest fear?

_____

_____

What would you order as your last meal?

_____

_____

_____

_____

Have you ever broken a bone? Which one(s) and how?

_____

_____

What is your favorite flower or plant?

_____

THE TEENAGE YEARS

"The scariest part of raising a teenager is remembering the things you did when you were a teenager." — Author Unknown

How would you describe yourself when you were a teenager?

_____

_____

_____

_____

How did you dress and style your hair during your teens?

_____

_____

_____

_____

_____

Did you hang out with a group or just a few close friends? Are you still close with any of them?

_____

_____

_____

_____

THE TEENAGE YEARS

"Teenagehood – that time in life when you show your
individuality by looking like everyone else." — Author Unknown

Describe a typical Friday or Saturday night during your high
school years.

_____

_____

_____

_____

Did you have a curfew?

_____

Did you date during your high school years?

_____

_____

Did you go to any school dances? What were they like?

_____

_____

_____

_____

Who taught you to drive and in what kind of car?

_____

_____

THE TEENAGE YEARS
"Little children, headache; big children, heartache."
— Italian Proverb

How old were you when you got your first car? What kind of car was it (year, make, and model)?

_____

_____

What school activities or sports did you participate in?

_____

_____

_____

_____

_____

What did you like and dislike about high school?

_____

_____

_____

_____

_____

_____

THE TEENAGE YEARS
"Keep true to the dreams of your youth."
— Friedrich Schiller

What were your grades like?

_____

_____

Did you have a favorite subject and a least favorite?

_____

_____

_____

What are a few favorite songs from your high school years?

_____

_____

_____

_____

_____

_____

_____

_____

THE TEENAGE YEARS

"Having a teenager can cause parents to wonder
about each other's heredity." — Author Unknown

Knowing all you know now, what advice would you give to
your teenage self? What might you have done differently in
school if you knew then what you know now?

_____

_____

_____

_____

_____

_____

_____

_____

_____

_____

_____

_____

_____

_____

THE TEENAGE YEARS

"Life is a winding path through hills and valleys and in
the end, the journey is all that matters." — Author Unknown

Write about a teacher, coach, or other mentor who had a
significant impact on you when you were growing up.

_____

_____

_____

_____

_____

_____

_____

_____

_____

_____

_____

_____

_____

BEGINNINGS
"We don't stop going to school when we graduate."
— Carol Burnett

What did you do after high school? Did you get a job, serve in the military, go to college or a trade school? Something else?

_____

_____

_____

_____

What led you to make this choice?

_____

_____

_____

_____

_____

If you went to college or trade school, what was your major/the focus of your education?

_____

_____

_____

BEGINNINGS
"it takes courage to grow up and become who you really are"
— ee cummings

How did this time period impact who you are today?

_____

_____

_____

_____

_____

If you could go back, what, if anything, would you change about this period of your life? Why?

_____

_____

_____

_____

_____

_____

_____

WORK & CAREER

"Even if you're on the right track, you'll get
run over if you just sit there." — Will Rogers

When you were a kid, what did you want to be when you grew up?

_____

_____

What was your first job? How old were you? How much were you paid?

_____

_____

How many jobs have you had during your lifetime? List a few of your favorites.

_____

_____

_____

_____

What is the least favorite job you have had?

_____

_____

_____

WORK & CAREER

"I'm a great believer in luck, and I find the harder
I work, the more I have of it." — Thomas Jefferson

Is there a job or profession your parents wanted you to
pursue? What was it?

_____

_____

_____

When people ask you what profession you are/were in, your
response is...

_____

_____

_____

How did you get into this career?

_____

_____

_____

_____

_____

_____

WORK & CAREER

"Choose a job you love and you will never
have to work a day in your life." — Confucius

What are/were the best parts of this profession?

_____

_____

_____

_____

_____

_____

_____

What aspects did you or do you dislike about it?

_____

_____

_____

_____

_____

_____

WORK & CAREER

"If people knew how hard I worked to get my mastery,
it wouldn't seem so wonderful after all." — Michelangelo

Who was the best boss you ever had? Why were they such a good manager?

_____

_____

_____

_____

_____

_____

What are some of your work and career-related achievements that you are proudest of?

_____

_____

_____

_____

_____

_____

_____

_____

TRIVIA

"Families are like branches on a tree. We grow in different
directions, yet our roots remain as one." — Author Unknown

Have you ever been told that you look like someone
famous? If yes, who?

_____

_____

_____

What is your morning routine?

_____

_____

_____

_____

What is a favorite guilty pleasure?

_____

_____

_____

Which television family most reminds you of your family
growing up?

_____

_____

TRIVIA

"What can you do to promote world peace?
Go home and love your family." — Mother Teresa

Did you have braces? If yes, how old were you when you got them?

_____

Do you like roller coasters?

_____

_____

What name would you choose if you had to change your first name?

_____

Did you ever skip school?

_____

If yes, did you get away with it and what did you do during the time you should have been in class?

_____

_____

_____

_____

_____

_____

FAMILY TREE

"Family is the most important thing in the world."
— Diana, Princess of Wales

My Great-Grandmother
(My Grandmother's Mom)

My Great-Grandmother
(My Grandfather's Mom)

My Great-Grandfather
(My Grandmother's Dad)

My Great-Grandfather
(My Grandfather's Dad)

My Grandmother
(My Mom's Mom)

My Grandfather
(My Mom's Dad)

My Mother

FAMILY TREE

"As you do for your ancestors, your children will do for you."
— African Proverb

My Great-Grandmother
(My Grandmother's Mom)

My Great-Grandmother
(My Grandfather's Mom)

My Great-Grandfather
(My Grandmother's Dad)

My Great-Grandfather
(My Grandfather's Dad)

My Grandmother
(My Dad's Mom)

My Grandfather
(My Dad's Dad)

My Father

PARENTS & GRANDPARENTS

"A man travels the world over in search of what he
needs and returns home to find it." — George A. Moore

Where was your mother born and where did she grow up?

_____

_____

_____

How would you describe her?

_____

_____

_____

In what ways are you most like your mother?

_____

_____

_____

_____

_____

_____

_____

_____

PARENTS & GRANDPARENTS

"Having somewhere to go is home. Having someone to love
is family. Having both is a blessing." — Author Unknown

Where was your father born and where did he grow up?

_____

_____

_____

How would you describe him?

_____

_____

_____

In what ways are you most like your father?

_____

_____

_____

_____

_____

_____

_____

_____

PARENTS & GRANDPARENTS
"A moment lasts for seconds but the memory of it lasts forever."
— Author Unknown

What is a favorite memory of your mother?

_____

_____

_____

_____

_____

_____

_____

_____

_____

_____

_____

_____

_____

_____

PARENTS & GRANDPARENTS
"We don't remember days, we remember moments."
— Author Unknown

What is a favorite memory of your father?

_____

_____

_____

_____

_____

_____

_____

_____

_____

_____

_____

_____

_____

_____

_____

PARENTS & GRANDPARENTS

"In every conceivable manner, the family is a link
to our past, bridge to our future." — Alex Haley

What was your mother's maiden name?

_____

Do you know from what part(s) of the world your mother's
family originates?

_____

_____

_____

Do you know your father's mother's maiden name?

_____

_____

Do you know from what part(s) of the world your father's
family originates?

_____

_____

_____

How did your parents meet?

_____

_____

_____

PARENTS & GRANDPARENTS

"Appreciate your parents. You never know what
sacrifices they went through for you." — Author Unknown

How would you describe their relationship?

_____

_____

_____

_____

_____

What were your parents' occupations?

_____

_____

_____

_____

Did either of them have any unique talents or skills?

_____

_____

_____

_____

Did either of them serve in the military?

_____

PARENTS & GRANDPARENTS

"Love is the chain whereby to bind a child to its parents."
— Abraham Lincoln

What is a favorite family tradition that was passed down from your parents or grandparents?

_____

_____

_____

What are a few of your favorite things that your mother or father would cook for the family?

_____

_____

_____

_____

What were your grandparents like on your mother's side?

_____

_____

_____

_____

_____

_____

PARENTS & GRANDPARENTS
"Next to God, thy parents."
— William Penn

Do you know where your mother's parents were born and grew up?

_____

_____

_____

_____

What were your grandparents like on your father's side?

_____

_____

_____

_____

_____

Do you know where your father's parents were born and grew up?

_____

_____

_____

PARENTS & GRANDPARENTS

"There is no school equal to a decent home and no
teacher equal to a virtuous parent." — Mahatma Gandhi

What is some of the best advice your mother gave you?

_____

_____

_____

_____

_____

_____

_____

_____

_____

_____

_____

_____

_____

PARENTS & GRANDPARENTS
"A father's goodness is higher than the mountain,
a mother's goodness deeper than the sea." — Japanese Proverb

What is some of the best advice your father gave you?

_____

_____

_____

_____

_____

_____

_____

_____

_____

_____

_____

_____

_____

_____

PARENTS & GRANDPARENTS

"My fathers planted for me, and I planted for my children."
— Hebrew Saying

Did you ever meet your great-grandparents on either side of your family? If yes, what were they like?

_____

_____

_____

_____

_____

_____

_____

_____

_____

_____

_____

_____

_____

PARENTS & GRANDPARENTS

"The longest road out is the shortest road home."
— Irish Proverb

What other individuals had a major role in helping you grow up?

_____

_____

_____

_____

_____

_____

_____

_____

_____

_____

_____

_____

_____

_____

YOUR SIBLINGS

"Brothers and sisters are as close as hands and feet."
— Vietnamese Saying

How many siblings do you have?

_____

Are you the oldest, middle, or youngest?

_____

List your siblings' names in order of their ages. Make sure to include yourself.

_____

_____

_____

_____

Which of your siblings were you the closest with growing up?

_____

_____

Which of your siblings are you the closest with in your adult years?

_____

_____

YOUR SIBLINGS

"The greatest gift our parents ever gave us was each other."
— Author Unknown

How would you describe each of your siblings when they were kids?

_____

_____

_____

_____

_____

_____

How would you describe each of your siblings as adults?

_____

_____

_____

_____

_____

_____

_____

YOUR SIBLINGS

"First a brother, then a bother, now a friend."
— Author Unknown

In the following pages, share some favorite memories of each of your siblings. If you're an only child, feel free to share memories of close friends or cousins.

_____

_____

_____

_____

_____

_____

_____

_____

_____

_____

_____

_____

YOUR SIBLINGS

"What causes sibling rivalry? Having more than one kid."
— Tim Allen

Memories...

_____

_____

_____

_____

_____

_____

_____

_____

_____

_____

_____

_____

_____

_____

YOUR SIBLINGS

"Siblings know how to push each other's buttons, but they also know how to mend things faster than anyone." — Author Unknown

Memories...

_____

_____

_____

_____

_____

_____

_____

_____

_____

_____

_____

_____

_____

YOUR SIBLINGS

"The advantage of growing up with siblings is that
you become very good at fractions." — Author Unknown

Memories...

_____

_____

_____

_____

_____

_____

_____

_____

_____

_____

_____

_____

_____

_____

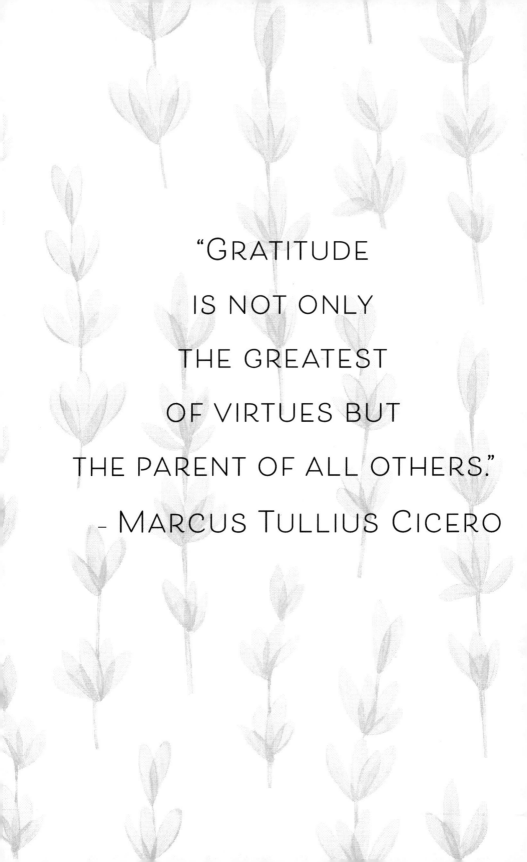

"GRATITUDE
IS NOT ONLY
THE GREATEST
OF VIRTUES BUT
THE PARENT OF ALL OTHERS."
- MARCUS TULLIUS CICERO

"LET US
BE GRATEFUL
TO PEOPLE
WHO MAKE US HAPPY;
THEY ARE
THE CHARMING GARDENERS
WHO MAKE
OUR SOULS BLOSSOM."
- MARCEL PROUST

TRIVIA

"Just when you think you know love, something little comes
along and reminds you just how big it is." — Author Unknown

If you could do any one thing for a day, what would it be?

_____

_____

_____

What is your favorite season? What are some things you
love about that time of the year?

_____

_____

_____

What is a smell that reminds you of your childhood? Why?

_____

_____

_____

What is your least favorite household chore?

_____

_____

What do you do better than anyone else in the family?

_____

_____

TRIVIA

"Always be a first-rate version of yourself and not a
second-rate version of someone else." — Judy Garland

What is your favorite dessert?

_____

What is a favorite memory from the last twelve months?

_____

_____

_____

_____

If you could only eat three things for the next year (with no
effect on your health), what would you pick?

_____

_____

_____

What is your definition of success?

_____

_____

_____

_____

_____

MORE ABOUT ME
"To find yourself, think for yourself."
— Socrates

What would you title your autobiography?

_____

_____

_____

What is your favorite quote?

_____

_____

_____

What are the main values you have tried to live your life by?

_____

_____

_____

_____

_____

_____

_____

_____

_____

MORE ABOUT ME

"The only journey is the journey within."
— Rainer Maria Rilke

What life experiences would you say have had the largest impact on who you are today?

_____

_____

_____

_____

_____

_____

_____

_____

_____

_____

_____

_____

_____

_____

MORE ABOUT ME
"Those who wish to sing, always find a song."
— Swedish Proverb

Who are the people who have had the largest impact on you becoming who you are today?

_____

_____

_____

_____

_____

_____

_____

_____

_____

_____

_____

_____

_____

MORE ABOUT ME

"The best way to predict your future is to create it."
— Abraham Lincoln

What are a few of your proudest personal accomplishments?

_____

_____

_____

_____

_____

_____

_____

_____

_____

_____

_____

_____

_____

MORE ABOUT ME

"The more you know yourself, the more patience you
have for what you see in others." — Erik Erikson

What is the hardest thing you have had to overcome in your
life?

_____

_____

_____

_____

_____

_____

_____

_____

_____

_____

_____

_____

_____

MORE ABOUT ME

"If the only prayer you ever say in your entire
life is thank you, it will be enough." — Meister Eckhart

Write about the decisions, actions, and people that helped
you succeed in overcoming this challenging time.

_____

_____

_____

_____

_____

_____

_____

_____

_____

_____

_____

_____

_____

_____

SPIRITUALITY & RELIGION

"Within you there is a stillness and a sanctuary to which
you can retreat at any time and be yourself." — Hermann Hesse

What do you believe is the purpose of life?

_____

_____

_____

_____

_____

_____

_____

_____

Which has the most impact on our lives: fate or free will?

_____

_____

_____

_____

_____

SPIRITUALITY & RELIGION
"What you are is God's gift to you, what you become
is your gift to God." — Hans Urs von Balthasar, Prayer

Were your parents religious when you were growing up? If
yes, how did they express their spiritual beliefs?

_____

_____

_____

_____

_____

_____

_____

_____

_____

_____

_____

_____

_____

SPIRITUALITY & RELIGION

"When I started counting my blessings, my
whole life turned around." — Willie Nelson

If you are religious or spiritual, how have your beliefs and
practices changed over the course of your life?

_____

_____

_____

_____

_____

_____

_____

_____

_____

_____

_____

_____

SPIRITUALITY & RELIGION

"Forgiveness does not change the past, but it
does enlarge the future." — Author Unknown

What religious or spiritual practices do you incorporate into
your daily life today, if any?

_____

_____

_____

_____

_____

_____

_____

Do you believe in miracles? Have you experienced one?

_____

_____

_____

_____

_____

_____

_____

SPIRITUALITY & RELIGION

"Don't be afraid your life will end; be afraid
that it will never begin." — Author Unknown

What do you do when times are challenging, and you need
to find additional inner strength?

_____

_____

_____

_____

_____

_____

_____

_____

_____

_____

_____

_____

SPIRITUALITY & RELIGION

"Cherish your yesterdays, dream your tomorrows
and live your todays." — Author Unknown

Write about a time you found relief by forgiving someone.

_____

_____

_____

_____

_____

_____

_____

_____

_____

_____

_____

_____

_____

_____

LOVE & ROMANCE
"We are asleep until we fall in love!"
— Leo Tolstoy, *War and Peace*

Do you believe in love at first sight?

_____

_____

_____

Do you believe in soulmates?

_____

_____

_____

How old were you when you had your first kiss?

_____

What age were you when you went on your first date?

_____

Can you remember who it was with and what you did?

_____

_____

_____

_____

_____

LOVE & ROMANCE

"Whatever our souls are made of, his and mine are the same."
— Emily Brontë, *Wuthering Heights*

How old were you when you had your first steady relationship? Who was it with?

_____

How many times in your life have you been in love?

_____

_____

What are some of the most important qualities of a successful relationship?

_____

_____

_____

_____

_____

_____

_____

_____

_____

LOVE & ROMANCE

"We loved with a love that was more than love."
— Edgar Allan Poe, *Annabel Lee*

Did you have any celebrity crushes when you were young?

_____

_____

_____

_____

Were you ever in a relationship with someone your parents did not approve of?

_____

_____

_____

Have you ever written someone or had someone write you a love poem or song?

_____

If yes, write a few lines that you may remember.

_____

_____

_____

_____

_____

LOVE & ROMANCE

"Love is a great beautifier."
— Louisa May Alcott, *Little Women*

In what ways do you feel your parents' relationship influenced how you have approached love and marriage?

_____

_____

_____

_____

_____

Write about a favorite romantic moment.

_____

_____

_____

_____

_____

_____

_____

_____

LOVE & ROMANCE
"Love loves to love love."
— James Joyce

How did you meet our uncle?

_____

_____

_____

_____

_____

What was your first impression of him?

_____

_____

_____

_____

_____

What is your proposal story?

_____

_____

_____

_____

LOVE & ROMANCE

"If I know what love is, it is because of you!"
— Hermann Hesse

What was your wedding like? Where was it held and who was there? Any good wedding day stories?

_____

_____

_____

_____

_____

_____

_____

_____

_____

_____

_____

_____

_____

TRAVEL

"Once a year, go someplace you've never been before."
— Dali Lama

Do you have a valid passport?

_____

How do you feel about cruises?

_____

_____

How do you feel about flying?

_____

What are a few of your favorite places that you've traveled to?

_____

_____

_____

_____

_____

_____

_____

_____

TRAVEL

"Life is short, and the world is wide."
— Author Unknown

What is a favorite travel memory?

_____

_____

_____

_____

_____

_____

_____

_____

_____

_____

_____

_____

_____

_____

TRAVEL BUCKET LIST

"Man cannot discover new oceans unless he has
the courage to lose sight of the shore." — André Gide

List the top 10 places you would visit if money and time
were no concern.

1. _____

_____

2. _____

_____

3. _____

_____

4. _____

_____

5. _____

_____

TRAVEL BUCKET LIST

"The world is a book, and those who do not
travel read only one page." — Saint Augustine

6. _____

_____

7. _____

_____

8. _____

_____

9. _____

_____

10. _____

_____

"EVERY

MOMENT

IS A

FRESH BEGINNING."

- T.S. ELIOT

"The best and most
beautiful things
in the world
cannot be
seen or even touched -
they must
be felt
with the heart."
- Helen Keller

LIFE MILESTONE MOMENTS

"When people throw stones at you, convert them into milestones."
— Author Unknown

Milestone Moments

When we look at our own life course, we will see times when our path has been smooth and unheeded and other stretches when it has been winding and uphill with stops and starts along the way.

We will also discover instances when our life path suddenly became harder – or easier – or went in a completely different direction.

These are those milestone moments, marks of time when we made a key decision, when something transformative happened to us, or when a goal we were working for was finally achieved.

Keeping these milestone moments fresh in our minds allows us to learn, to grow, to give thanks, and to celebrate. This awareness makes us stronger and more understanding of the fact that one single day can change everything.

Remembering and knowing that a single choice or a single day can change everything helps us cherish all the days of our lives. We become more willing to make hard choices and take positive risks.

We become brave in our goals, and we work harder to achieve them. We see more of our self-value, and we make ourselves and our ambitions a priority.

LIFE MILESTONE MOMENTS
"A milestone is less date and more definition."
— Rands

A milestone moment I can identify in my life is...

_____

_____

_____

What were the circumstances that led up to this moment?

_____

_____

_____

What were the changes to you and your life that came from this milestone moment?

_____

_____

_____

_____

_____

_____

_____

LIFE MILESTONE MOMENTS

"Remember to celebrate milestones as you
prepare for the road ahead." — Nelson Mandela

What is a second milestone moment from your life that you
can think of?

_____

_____

_____

What were the circumstances that led up to this moment?

_____

_____

_____

What were the changes to you and your life that came from
this milestone moment?

_____

_____

_____

_____

_____

_____

LIFE MILESTONE MOMENTS

"Sometimes the hardest thing and the right
thing are the same thing." — Author Unknown

What is a third milestone moment from your life that you can
think of?

_____

_____

_____

What were the circumstances that led up to this moment?

_____

_____

_____

What were the changes to you and your life that came from
this milestone moment?

_____

_____

_____

_____

_____

_____

_____

POLITICAL STUFF

"Each person must live their life as a model for others."
— Rosa Parks

Which best describes how you feel about having political discussions:

☐ I would rather not.
☐ I prefer to have them with people whose views match mine.
☐ I love a good debate.

How old were you the first time you voted?

_____

What are the biggest differences in your political views today and when you were in your early twenties?

_____

_____

_____

_____

_____

Have you ever taken part in a march or boycott? What issues, if any, could motivate you to join one?

_____

_____

_____

_____

POLITICAL STUFF

"In politics stupidity is not a handicap."
— Napoleon Bonaparte

When was the last time you voted?

_____

In what ways do you agree and disagree with the political choices of younger generations?

_____

_____

_____

_____

_____

_____

If you woke up to find yourself in charge of the country, what are the first three things you would enact or change?

One: _____

_____

Two: _____

_____

Three: _____

_____

MOVIES, MUSIC, TELEVISION, & BOOKS

"If you want a happy ending, that depends, of course, on where you stop your story." — Orson Welles

What movie have you watched the greatest number of times?

_____

_____

What movie or television show can you remember loving when you were a kid?

_____

_____

Who would you cast to play yourself in the movie of your life? How about for the rest of your family?

_____

_____

_____

_____

_____

_____

_____

MOVIES, MUSIC, TELEVISION, & BOOKS

"In three words I can sum up everything I've learned about life: it goes on." — Robert Frost

What are your favorite genres of music?

_____

_____

_____

_____

Which decades had the best music?

_____

_____

_____

_____

What is the first record (or cassette, cd, etc.) you can remember buying or being given as a gift?

_____

_____

What song do you like today that would make your younger self cringe?

_____

_____

MOVIES, MUSIC, TELEVISION, & BOOKS

"Only the gentle are ever really strong."
— James Dean

What is a song from your teens that reminds you of a special event or moment?

_____

_____

_____

What song would you pick as the theme song of your life?

_____

_____

_____

What was the first concert you attended? Where was it held and when?

_____

_____

How has your taste in music changed over the years?

_____

_____

_____

_____

MOVIES, MUSIC, TELEVISION, & BOOKS

"Life is a flower of which love is the honey."
— Victor Hugo

What television show from the past do you wish was still on the air?

_____

If you could be cast in any television show or movie, past or present, which one would you choose?

_____

What are some favorite books from your childhood and/or teenage years?

_____

_____

_____

What book or books have majorly impacted the way you think, work, or live your life?

_____

_____

_____

_____

_____

TOP TEN MOVIES

"Adults are just outdated children."
— Dr. Seuss

List up to ten of your most favorite movies:

1. _____

2. _____

3. _____

4. _____

5. _____

6. _____

7. _____

8. _____

9. _____

10. _____

TOP TEN SONGS

"The music is not in the notes, but in the silence in between."
— Wolfgang Amadeus Mozart

List up to ten of your most favorite songs:

1. _____

2. _____

3. _____

4. _____

5. _____

6. _____

7. _____

8. _____

9. _____

10. _____

TOP TEN TELEVISION SHOWS

"Television is simply automated day-dreaming."
— Lee Lovinger

List up to ten of your most favorite television shows:

1. _____

2. _____

3. _____

4. _____

5. _____

6. _____

7. _____

8. _____

9. _____

10. _____

TOP TEN BOOKS

"A room without books is like a body without a soul."
— Cicero

List up to ten of your most favorite books:

1. _____

2. _____

3. _____

4. _____

5. _____

6. _____

7. _____

8. _____

9. _____

10. _____

TRIVIA

"The way I see it, if you want the rainbow,
you gotta put up with the rain." — Dolly Parton

If you could travel through time and had to choose, who would you meet: your ancestors or your descendants? Why?

_____

_____

_____

_____

What are five things you are grateful for?

_____

_____

_____

_____

Who would you invite if you could have dinner with any five people who have ever lived?

_____

_____

_____

_____

TRIVIA

"Life is a succession of lessons which must
be lived to be understood." — Helen Keller

If you were forced to sing karaoke, what song would you
perform?

_____

_____

What is your favorite holiday and why?

_____

_____

_____

_____

_____

Which ten-year period of your life has been your favorite so
far and why?

_____

_____

_____

_____

_____

ROOM FOR MORE
"Not until we are lost do we begin to understand ourselves."
— Henry David Thoreau

The following pages are for you to expand on some of your answers, to share more memories, and/or to write notes to your loved ones:

_____

_____

_____

_____

_____

_____

_____

_____

_____

_____

_____

_____

_____

ROOM FOR MORE

"When you cease to dream you cease to live."
— Malcom Forbes

_____

_____

_____

_____

_____

_____

_____

_____

_____

_____

_____

_____

_____

_____

ROOM FOR MORE

"Without music, life would be a blank to me."
— Jane Austen, *Emma*

_____

_____

_____

_____

_____

_____

_____

_____

_____

_____

_____

_____

_____

ROOM FOR MORE

"Where words fail, music speaks."
— Hans Christian Andersen

_____

_____

_____

_____

_____

_____

_____

_____

_____

_____

_____

_____

_____

ROOM FOR MORE

"What is unforgiven from yesterday will define who
and how we are tomorrow." — Author Unknown

_____

_____

_____

_____

_____

_____

_____

_____

_____

_____

_____

_____

_____

ROOM FOR MORE

"Life is a great big canvas, and you should throw
all the paint on it you can." — Danny Kaye

ROOM FOR MORE

"The difference between who you are and who
you want to be is what you do." — Author Unknown

ROOM FOR MORE

"Life isn't about finding yourself.
Life is about creating yourself." — Chinese Saying

_____

_____

_____

_____

_____

_____

_____

_____

_____

_____

_____

_____

_____

_____

ROOM FOR MORE

"Enough is a feast."
— Buddhist Proverb

_____

_____

_____

_____

_____

_____

_____

_____

_____

_____

_____

_____

_____

_____

_____

ROOM FOR MORE

"Be – don't try to become."
— Osho

_____

_____

_____

_____

_____

_____

_____

_____

_____

_____

_____

_____

_____

_____

HEAR YOUR STORY BOOKS

At **Hear Your Story**, we have created a line of books focused on giving each of us a place to tell the unique story of who we are, where we have been, and where we are going.

Sharing and hearing the stories of the people in our lives creates a closeness and understanding, ultimately strengthening our bonds.

Available at Amazon, all bookstores, and HearYourStory.com

- Dad, I Want to Hear Your Story: A Father's Guided Journal to Share His Life & His Love

- Mom, I Want to Hear Your Story: A Mother's Guided Journal to Share Her Life & Her Love

- Grandfather, I Want to Hear Your Story: A Grandfather's Guided Journal to Share His Life and His Love

- Grandmother, I Want to Hear Your Story: A Grandmother's Guided Journal to Share Her Life and Her Love

- You Choose to Be My Dad; I Want to Hear Your Story: A Guided Journal for Stepdads to Share Their Life Story

- Life Gave Me You; I Want to Hear Your Story: A Guided Journal for Stepmothers to Share Their Life Story

HEAR YOUR STORY BOOKS

- To My Wonderful Aunt, I Want to Hear Your Story: A Guided Journal to Share Her Life and Her Love

- To My Uncle, I Want to Hear Your Story: A Guided Journal to Share His Life and His Love

- The Story of Expecting You: A Selfcare Pregnancy Guided Journal and Memory Book

- Because I Love You: The Couple's Bucket List That Builds Your Relationship

- To My Boyfriend, I Want to Hear Your Story

- To My Girlfriend, I Want to Hear Your Story

- Love Notes: I Wrote This Book About You

- Getting to Know You: 201 Fun Questions to Deepen Your Relationship and Hear Each Other's Story

- You, Me, and Us: 229 Fun Relationship Questions to Ask Your Guy or Girl

- Papá, quiero oír tu historia: El diario guiado de un padre Para compartir su vida y su amor

- Mamá, quiero oír tu historia: El diario guiado de un padre Para compartir su vida y su amor

ABOUT THE AUTHOR

Jeffrey Mason was raised in a small town in Texas, leaving to serve as a Hospital Corpsman with the United States Navy and Marine Corps.

The first 12 years of his working life was in healthcare, followed by twenty plus years working with businesses, government agencies, couples, and individuals.

From there he "retired" to write and publish books.

He has two adult children and today lives with his wife and their cats in Sacramento, California. When he isn't writing, he enjoys cooking, gardening, and traveling.

To date, Jeffrey has written 23 books, mostly centered around the discovery and sharing of personal and family histories.

This focus inspired him to create **Hear Your Story**, a company with the mission to make it simple for anyone to reminisce and share the stories of their life, while also creating a cherished memory that can be shared for generations.

For every book sold, **Hear Your Story** donates twenty-five cents to non-profit organizations. To date, these contributions have benefitted Alzheimer's research and care, domestic violence prevention, and helping kids and teenagers manage depression and social anxiety.

You can contact Jeffrey directly at hello@jeffreymason.com or through his two websites: https://hearyourstory.com and https://www.jeffreymason.com.

He would be grateful if you would help people to find his books by leaving a review on Amazon. Your feedback helps him get better at this thing he loves.

VIEW THIS BOOK
ON YOUR COMPUTER

We invite you to also check out HearYourStory.com, where you can answer the questions in this book using your smart phone, tablet, or computer.

Answering the questions online at HearYourStory.com allows you to write as much as you want, to save your responses and revisit and revise them whenever you wish, and to print as many copies as you need for you and your whole family.

Please note there is a small one-time charge to cover the cost of maintaining the site.

ISBN: 978-1-955034-46-3

Made in the USA
Las Vegas, NV
22 December 2024

ae056be9-0581-4450-bf1a-8372bfc3a2ccR02